THE MINE

MINING FOR THE PURE ESSENCE OF THE INNER YOU

By: Ranikka Jones

Unless otherwise noted, all scripture is from the KingJames Version of the Bible.

First printing, 2021.

Table of Contents

Preface

Diamonds are viewed as one of the most beautiful and sought-after possessions on Earth, but rarely does anyone talk about the caves, high temperatures, or the amount of time and pressure that comes with the territory of becoming a diamond. Diamonds are astonishing to admire, but the process of it receiving its identity is far from pretty. The proper process for a diamond to be formed is that it must be buried in the depths of the earth or in caves in the wilderness. The Mine is a collective body of art that depicts the journey through some of my life's most challenging caves.

I dwelt in a cave for many years, living a life of darkness and confusion, and crawling into tight spaces that sometimes left me gasping for air. My cave was dirty and cold, and left me with identity loss, confidence battles and self-worth issues. This wasn't a literal cave, but a cave of relationship disappointments and setbacks. At times, my life was so dark that I felt like that was the best life had to offer. But, one day, I found light and that light was the beginning of my life. I'm no longer a cave dweller. Living life to the fullest is my goal.

I figure the best way to explain my experience is to guide you through the debris that once laid molded on the floor of my heart until I took the necessary steps to reconstruct life as I knew it. As your tour guide, I pray upon the completion of this exploration you are introduced or re-introduced to the hidden treasure that awaits you!

You have now entered The Mine.

Entrance: Watch Your Step

"Smile for the camera, Ranikka," were five words that echoed in my ears for years - like after having a loud fun-filled night with your girls at your favorite night club. As a child, I had nonchalantly accepted that if I smiled and waved this would serve as a quick fix for how I felt internally. I wasn't properly shown how to express my emotions, so it would unintentionally come off as an attitude.

Those two overlooked mindsets took me years of digging to find the root of my unwillingness to communicate or the need for periodic emotional breakdowns. We will take a closer look at that later, but it's needed for our first cave. Okay? Back to my early years.

I was the kid who was raved over and slowly molded into the trophy child, so that meant I was extremely protected.

That occurs when you're the first child and a girl. DOUBLE PROTECTION, right? Hey, I'm not saying I didn't work hard on my own, but I fed off the constant attention and rewards of being a well-behaved little princess. The downfall of that was having approval seeking and validation issues as a teenager and adult because I was so ignorant of who I was without it.

It's crazy how people can look so PERFECT on paper, but at the core, they can be dumbfounded about life and how to maneuver through it. That person was me. Oh, don't leave me with my hand up by myself. We are already in the dirt, so let's get dirtier!

Cave 1: You Got Potential

It was my senior year of high school and as the school year came to an end, chanting "SENIORS 2008" with the rest of my fellow graduates seemed normal on the outside, but on the inside, I was using my excitement to hide the disgust of allowing someone in one of my most secret chambers during the last year of one of the most important times of my life. Shortly after that came the personal put downs. "You're so stupid girl!" "It wasn't even what you expected. Now look at you!"

These are the phrases I said to myself to side-step the truth. I was trying to explain away my actions about everything and refusing to face the truth head on. I literally felt like a bag of dirt, and along with that, I was ashamed that I ruined this streak of having it all together.

See, for almost my whole life up until this point, I had done nothing but be the perfect trophy child my environment instilled in me to be, and after 20 plus years, this was the TOUGHEST chain to break for me. I can't lie. It seeped into my pores like an injection and slowly started causing a reaction that was in dire need of a prescription. I found myself inhaling and exhaling this nasty lie of perfection like it was oxygen, but if you had asked me, I thought it was WHO I WAS! The thing is, I later found out that I was leaning on a lower understanding of what I felt perfection was instead of leaning into who God said I WAS.

Proverbs 3:5-6

"Trust in the LORD with all thine heart; and lean not unto thine own understanding. In all thy ways acknowledge him, and he shall direct thy paths."

Roaming throughout life with this misconception of my true identity eventually led me to allowing people to treat me as a doormat. I believe we all have experienced moments of feeling weak, and in an effort to feel some sort of emotional connection, we let people do as they please. This false reality also followed me throughout my college years, and honestly it was one of the most dreadful, unfulfilling times of my life.

Those moments of unpleasantness came from the constant search for approval, living in fear of making mistakes or wanting to belong even if that acceptance didn't have my best interest at heart. The thing is, I never took out the time to get acquainted with myself, but I was besties with this fraud version of myself. Why do we live our lives at the expense of our authenticity and peace?

I believe we sometimes shun away from what doesn't bring us a sense of comfort and being myself was something I wasn't willing to dwell in. I was literally terrified of my own potential because I wasn't aware of how simply being me would one day change me completely.

One thing about not knowing your potential is that it will reveal your weaknesses and unveil you to another world if you're not strong enough. So, due to my lack of knowledge of who I was I started to find myself detaching from life and things I once enjoyed during my earlier years in college. I started distancing myself from family & loved ones, lacked mental focus on my academics, stopped attending church and arrived at a place of simply not caring about anything but myself. Here I am with this bright potential but I'm sweeping it under the rug because of my insecurities, selfish ways and pressure to be liked instead of respected. It came at a cost I couldn't afford to pay.

I found myself looking at an unrecognizable scared little girl in the mirror who allowed the temptations of this newfound popularity, lit college parties, and handsome guys to reach out to me based on their convenience. (Oh, I had my choice of contacts & I was thrilled about it) I gave and gave myself until I was left empty.

I exerted so much energy basking in this distorted reality that I never allowed the essence of who I was to flourish. As I look back on that phase in my life, I would tell that version of myself that she's more than enough and accepted by the King of Kings!

The thing about potential is normally others see it before you, and they can deter you from ever embracing it if you let them. This was a prime example of why being mindful of the company you keep is important because you become a reflection of them.

It's important to surround yourself with people who build you up, have genuine sincerity towards you and want to see you elevate in your walk-through life. It shouldn't just be a receiving interaction, but you should be a giver of the same energy. If someone is in your life, find time to examine their intentions because bad company can be deceitful. It wasn't just their fault but also mine because I didn't have the right motives of pursuing those kinds of friendships.

This cave allowed me to spot out the kind of people I needed to remove myself from and the kind of people I needed to be a part of my life. To this day, I'm extremely blessed with the connections I made during that transition in my life.

However, I buried that part of my life for years and never wanted to relive it because of the embarrassment and pain it caused me. One of the biggest parts of that embarrassment was the fact that I was getting entangled with guys who I should've never given the time of day. But, as stated at the beginning of this tour, I desired validation and wanted to feel the pleasures of being wanted.

Queens, let me tell you, do not lower your standards for the approval of someone who doesn't appreciate your worth. You are not a random toy for a guy to pick up and put down at his leisure. You are deserving of someone who views you as royalty and handles you with care.

If someone would've told me this at that point in my life, I would've laughed at them. I never realized this because what my surroundings were showing me cause me to lower my standards and not value myself. It might've baited guys but that didn't make them stay.

Based on the entrance of this cave you would've thought I learned my lesson about who I was involving myself with and decided to try a different path right?

To be transparent with you, I didn't know who the heck I was because I had always lived in the shadows of being a counterfeit.

So, it was easy to continue to fall prey to the enemy's trap that he set up for my life. Until one day, I grew tired of my own mess and knew that I was better than what I was letting off to be. If I wasn't doing it for the present me, I had to make the adjustment for the future me.

Listen sis, you have permission to change the direction of your life and seek out a better outcome whenever you decide to even if you feel like you've fallen short of your own potential a thousand times.

The amazing thing about falling short is you have the POTENTIAL to get back up again!

Proverbs 24:16

"For a just man falleth seven times, and riseth again."

Tell me, do you see yourself in this cave of the journey I experienced? If so, stay close because we are moving deeper into the cave, but here are a few affirmations I want you to stop and say the following affirmations aloud.

Affirmations:

"I will no longer hold myself hostage to my past, former identities, or anything else that doesn't represent God's will for my life!"

"I will be in the company of those who help me maximize my potential and not diminish it."

"I will take the opportunity to become acquainted with the beauty of who I am."

"I will stop lowering my standards for short term satisfaction from people or things."

"I will forgive myself for knowingly and unknowingly putting myself in situations that aren't beneficial to me."

Cave 2: Angel in Disguise

As I mentioned during the process of accepting my potential, I quickly realized I was still lost and needed to pick up the pieces of my life. I thought I needed something or someone to help me find my way back to my happy place. One thing you should never do is try to find void fillers in people or things that God didn't call you to. This is exactly how I landed myself in the devil's playground because I wasn't guarding my heart or filling every area in my life with good vibes.

I discovered myself taking interest in a guy who I assumed was different because he checked every box on my list. First off, his approach seemed sincere because he actually took an interest in me and not what I could do for him. Secondly, I felt safe and seen in his presence. However, one thing I didn't check off my list is if he was capable of showing me the utmost respect. But, how can we expect someone to hold us to a high esteem if we don't respect ourselves? My self-worth was in shambles when I met him but escaping how I truly felt about myself was all that mattered to me at the time.

I was head over heels for the potential of someone who wasn't even as interested in me as I was in him. What is it about a charming personality and a killer smile that makes us lose all the brain cells in our head's ladies? This was exactly what happened in this situation that would change everything about how I looked at men.

Men are meant to be protectors, but this attachment made me feel anything but protected as we continued dating. Due to this I started to assume maybe I wasn't worthy of experiencing the safeness of a man. I had the mentality that thought, “At least I have a man, so I better take what I get”.

In the end, my eagerness to be loved and naive ways continued to lead me down a swirling path of constant heartache and unfulfilled promises. I was nineteen years old and still exploring life. I now see the deception I signed up for when I decided to attach myself to someone I only knew on the surface.

Overall, this wasn’t a go out on dates, meet your Mama kind of situation, sis. Let’s just call it what it is: A SITUATIONSHIP. I’ve learned you can’t cook your way, sex your way or even talk your way into forcing someone to commit to you. A man knows if he wants to pursue you and if his actions aren’t lining up, there’s your answer. If you find yourself ever dealing with a guy and the conversation of intentional dating isn’t discussed…RUN!

A man without you in his future plans is a man who will plan to get away with whatever he can.

Since I didn't set any boundaries, I opened the door for the enemy to deceive me into thinking I'd found the one. I thought things were going so well for a long time, and I felt like the most beautiful girl in the world having this very attractive guy in my life. He was meeting me after classes, calling me every day and even throwing down in the kitchen. I felt like I had hit the jackpot. Until one day the jackpot slammed me into a wall after I confronted him about his dishonesty with talking to another person. At the time, I thought since we had a fling, he was entitled to me.

I vividly remember arriving at his place and waiting in the back for him to finish dinner. Something felt off but I downplayed it. Now I know it was God warning me.

After we finished eating, I revealed what I found out. The next thing I remember is hearing this tone and seeing this expression on his face that frightened me. It felt sinister and I wanted to get myself out of that situation as fast as I could. In the blink of a moment, I felt myself being thrown into the wall and told to never question what he did again.

All I can remember after that is running out of that house, jumping in my vehicle, and driving into a mailbox just to get away. Far away is where I wanted to be. As soon as I made it safely home, I blocked his number and changed routes the next day to avoid any future contact with him.

I know you're thinking, "Girl, why didn't you tell someone or press charges?" I was too embarrassed and was still trying to keep up this image of perfection. Plus, my family would have done some serious damage to him. The last straw was when he started stalking me until I had to threaten him with the law. His actions should have told me the accusations of being bipolar and disrespectful to women were true, but I was too blinded by his charming words and wasn't using any kind of wisdom about the situation.

Thankfully, I was eventually able to get completely free of this situation by accepting the fact that I was not using discernment. I ended up cutting off all communication with him, showing him forgiveness as well as myself and making myself completely unavailable so I could start my healing process.

Ephesians 5:6

"Let no one deceive you with empty words, for because of such things God's wrath comes on those who are disobedient."

That situationship also gave me the strength I needed to remove myself from that dangerous entanglement, and

I started to get my focus back. I began to start remembering why I came to college and decided to become an active participant in different organizations.

My self-confidence and self-worth blossomed too along that healing journey because I didn't need affirmation from anyone about who I was and how I deserve to be treated. I took time away from pursuing relationships and started dating my priorities.

Then boom! Shortly after I settled into my new found confidence, I met someone who would forever change my life for the better in the most bittersweet way. I believe God gives us the opportunity to meet people on Earth who are like angels in disguise.

I'm a firm believer in meeting people in your life journey who are meant to teach you lessons and this new guy did exactly that. We met at a time where I was starting to gain clarity of who I wanted to grow into but didn't quite know how to completely remove myself from the past.

I was still wearing my mistakes like a "Hello My Name Is" badge but the beautiful thing about him was that he overlooked all of my scars and saw the depths of my heart. That was the first time since being a child that I felt comfortable and safe to be myself around a man. The experience felt like I was a part of a Hallmark Movie, and we know how romantic those movies can be right?

Being able to let my guard down and allow someone to care about me was an extremely vulnerable moment in my life. How could someone want to love me in the midst of my flaws? I didn't think I was worthy. I felt like DAMAGED GOODS. The truth I know now is that I was more than worthy of experiencing a sincere love because the purity of my heart attracted me to him.

We talked about our lives and being able to live our wildest dreams. To my surprise, he became one of my biggest supporters, but all of that changed in an instant.

One minute I was on cloud nine, and the next minute I felt like I was falling 100 mph off that cloud. I received some of the worst news in my life. This man who had been able to open my eyes up to life, could no longer open his. My life immediately felt like it was a vapor, and I wanted to disappear with him. One of my dearest friends was gone, and I never got an opportunity to truly tell him how he changed my life. He showed me a gentle nature of a man that I never witnessed before, and he didn't expect perfection out of me.

The way he built me up even when my own reflection was telling me differently. The level of patience to care for me and want to learn how to love me was sincere. We discussed our futures together and I knew this was someone I would be happy to take a step towards purpose with. The thing is, we often cross paths with people that are good for us, but we aren't in the right place to fully receive what they can offer.

This moment haunted me for years because I felt the guilt of not being as vulnerable with him as he was towards me. He was an angel in disguise, and I will always cherish the memories we shared.

If you take anything from this cave, learn to treat every person who you're blessed to have in your life with appreciation. You never know who God may send to serve as a blessing in your life. If you have a disagreement, be quick to forgive, and don't allow bitterness to take root in your heart. Make sure you tell those you care for how much you love them. It's those simple things that make the difference.

Before we leave this particular cave, I also want you to know that you're worthy of experiencing a love that feels like it came from heaven itself. I know it's possible. Believe me! I lived and experienced it for myself through my guardian angel.

Take a moment and say these affirmations aloud.

Affirmations:

"I will ALWAYS be sure to let my true feelings be known for those I care for."

"I will NEVER allow myself to be treated inferior because God has called us to be Royalty."

"I will BE AWARE of a person's inner spirit more than the outer surface."

"I WILL forgive myself."

"I will BE ABLE to move on after loss because there's always a lesson in it."

"I will allow myself to accept love no matter who I've experienced because I'm worthy of it."

"I will not self-sabotage any good thing that enters my life because of fear of the unknown."

"I will learn to appreciate every person who is sent into my life."

Cave 3: The High Life

As I finally began trying to move forward after that last season of my life, I spent many long nights partying, missing classes because I couldn't focus and dating guys again that I KNEW I would never have a future with. I needed an INTERVENTION.

I had lost every sense of reality because I was so caught up in this false world of grief that I wanted to dwell in. I was searching for this void to be desperately filled by everything else but the ONE who could fill it…which was God.

To be honest, I was naive and so far from God at that point in my life. I felt so disgusted. Overlooked. A doormat. I had no idea that I was falling into a state of depression and loneliness until it was too late. No one could tell on the outside because I hid it so well, but it showed through my lack of eating and sleeping while I increased my drinking, smoking, profanity and more. I was hurting and this was my cry for help, but no one answered. I had to find the courage to change the narrative of my story myself. I knew if I didn't start improving my life, I could possibly lose everything including myself.

Psalm 139:14

"I praise you, for I am fearfully and wonderfully made. Wonderful are your works; my soul knows it very well."

The courage that I needed finally began to manifest once I began to accept the passing of my dear friend. I started to really take the time to see what he saw in me, but the questions I kept wondering to myself were, "Why did it take me so long?" and, "How come I didn't receive those constant reminders of my worth? I noticed that I didn't understand the value of affirming yourself and not depending on that validation when someone else affirms you.

I began to see that real confidence is when you can speak these affirmations into yourself because you believe it for you.

During this time, I also realized that because I was disobedient and wanted to live my life like I wanted, I had to endure the hardships of living the high life. It was by no means an easy season, but I'm grateful that I escaped this dangerous lifestyle.

My definition of the high life is any activity you incorporate into your life to assist you with escaping your current one, and I went on an escaping spree for a long time until I could no longer run. I had to wake up, face the facts, and take responsibility for my actions.

The beauty of this time was that it allowed me to use those lessons as fuel to do better and provided me with consistent self-worth reminders.

I started back focusing on my academics, removed myself from circles that didn't uplift me and started walking towards a path that would be one of the first YES's I've ever given myself.

During this phase of discovering my purpose in life again, I graduated from college, found a passion for pursuing my artistry, and started getting in shape while enjoying life post grad. Those were some of the most memorable times of my life, and I realized that being able to experience those moments was the real high.

Affirmations:

"I WILL always remember that I'm worthy of feeling worthy."

"I will NO LONGER connect myself to anything that doesn't represent who I AM now."

"I will say YES to me even if it hurts and is outside of my normal.

Cave 4: Crazy in Love

Years passed during my journey of bettering myself and while I was literally minding my own business. I met another guy, and I fell in love so it seemed. It felt like I was in the middle of a Queen Bey anthem. You know she has a good one for almost every situation.

One day, I got a notification on Facebook from someone inquiring about my music. At the time I was focused on continuing along this path of bettering myself, and I was happy with life. However, somewhere between the inquiry and a few weeks passing we found ourselves communicating more outside of just the music.

When our friendship started it was strictly based on business, but it shifted into a relationship I never saw coming. The next thing I knew we were in a relationship that caught me off guard, and to be honest, I wasn't truly ready for it.

If I could leave you with some advice, it would be to never agree to something you're not ready for. This relationship happened because I was afraid to tell him I wasn't ready for a serious relationship. Here I am again in another situation I should've taken my time with.

In the beginning, it took me a while to fully open up to him because of my past relationships, but with time, I started finding my walls of self-protection coming down. We became INSEPARABLE, which could be a good thing and a bad thing depending on how you view it.

Need I remind you; I was doing my thing when he came along, but I found myself losing grips on reality again. I know you're probably wondering, "How sis?"

Long story short, I noticed myself prioritizing him over me, neglecting the possible red flags and losing focus of what I worked so hard on building back up again…which was myself.

These next few steps are important, and I want you to recognize them early on so you can be careful, okay? After almost losing myself for the umpteenth time to another relationship, I was able to get out of this one early on before it took me to rock bottom again, but I definitely understand the importance of pointing out these common mistakes that are the least talked about amongst women when it comes to dating and being in relationships.

The "No-No's of Being a Girlfriend"

First things first, say "NO" to being entangled with anyone who will take you off your God given course. If this person isn't leading you closer to God, your purpose or even closer together as a couple, he has no business leading you anywhere at all.

Secondly, you have to say "NO" to becoming so overtaken by your significant other that you forget about YOU! At the end of the day, you matter and implementing self-care regimens for your wellbeing is a necessity.

Thirdly, you have to say "NO" to feeling like you are "responsible" to financially invest in someone who isn't your husband or wife. If you're not being led by God to give someone monetary gifts, you shouldn't do it because you're not bound together by a covenant union.

Fourthly, you have to to say "NO" to getting in somebody's kitchen slaving like you're their wife or involving yourself in domestic tasks. Don't feel obligated to cook for someone just because you're dating. Picnic outings or restaurant dates can serve as an option outside of cooking.

Fifthly, you have to say "NO" to giving your temple away for a temporary pleasure that won't keep your relationship together. The best way is to seek God and be yoked with someone who shares your same beliefs on sex and is willing to abstain until marriage.

Lastly, you have to say "NO" to yoking up with someone who God didn't call you to. By staying in God's presence and learning how to love yourself properly you will find it easier to not fall so quickly for just anyone.

At the end of the day, we cared about each other a lot in that relationship, but something within me kept telling me this wasn't suitable for me. I tried to leave, but sometimes the heart wants what the heart wants, and I wanted him!

Oftentimes, I looked back and wished I followed God's lead that was telling me to leave him alone because later on I found that the decision to stay eventually hurt me more.

Let's stop for a moment before we dive into that part of the story and say our affirmations.

Affirmations:

"I WILL remember to keep my heart in mind."

"I WILL be a better steward of my body, emotions, finances, and God's blessings."

"I WILL always check with God about my current relationship status or future relationship."

Cave 5: Built In Fear

In my mind, I thought being shown off, flown out, loved on and posted on the Gram would qualify me to be my entanglement from the last chapter's wife. I was SO WRONG!

We continued in this relationship that I knew wasn't right, but I realized that I was fighting for a love that didn't transfer to the other person. It was devestating.

Within those three years, I experienced all the highs, the lows and the hardships of trying to fight for our relationship. To be honest, God's voice was getting louder and louder telling me to leave, but despite it all, I wasn't ready to play the role of a single woman again.

I was so used to settling and neglecting how I felt at that point, that those traits had become part of my nature. I even knew other women found him attractive and played petty games whenever I was around to get the best reaction out of me. Take it from me sis, you have to watch how someone makes you feel in public because there's no telling what they're doing behind your back.

The longer we were together, the more desperate I became for reassurance because I suffered from abandonment issues and constantly needed to know I was the best girlfriend he ever had. In reality I was just bitter, cold hearted and jealous because I knew in my heart that I wasn't loving myself properly and I deserved better than what I was settling for.

What that taught me was that someone will only treat you the way you treat yourself. My insecurities were connected to his insecurities. Our toxicity and unhealed childhoods were married…that's the real reason we came together. Yes, it's true you can care about someone deeply but not be a good fit. We connected because our spirits were battered from our past experiences with wanting to be loved and it created a soul tie. Sometimes, our hearts want what it wants but that doesn't mean it's what we need. Compatibility is an important factor in a relationship, and it should happen naturally.

This was the part of my story when I realized I needed to walk away or this relationship would break me. When you're with someone for a lengthy amount of time, it's hard to imagine your life without them. My last straw came the night we had the most heated argument within the 3 years of being a couple. At that time, I had an extra phone that I allowed him to use while he worked on getting a new one. The time came when he got a new phone, but I didn't receive mine back. One night I told him I'll reset the phone as soon as I got mine back. The real reason is because I wanted to catch him in a lie because I wanted to prove myself right. He refused to return the phone and items were thrown and hurtful words were exchanged. This wasn't the road I wanted to travel again.

Listen Sis, I wasn't perfect either because at the time I was bitter and always wanted the last say. I caused some of the toxicity as well, and that's why I realized I still wasn't fit for a relationship. I had this mentality, "Oh you hurt me. Well, I'll hurt you back worse. Looking back, most of that entire relationship was based off of sex if I'm being honest, and we never truly opened up about our inner battles. Eventually, I learned that those feelings go away, and you become numb to the toxicity. The question I had to ask myself was, "Is it really worth your heart Ranikka?

The things we worried about the most were what people would think if we broke up, and I began to forget who I was before he came along. Who are we really? What would people think if we broke up? Who was I before you?

Sis, the main thing I want to let you know before we start moving forward on this tour, is not to create a love based off of insecurities but create a love based off of love itself, which is God, and the love you have within yourself.

Say our next set of affirmations aloud.

Affirmations:

"I WILL not ignore any signs that are sent as a warning for my safety and my well-being."

"I WILL always be aware of getting to know someone before I jump into a relationship."

"I WILL always work on speaking well of someone even if we are no longer together."

"I WILL be responsible for my healing and not look for my deliverance in anybody or anything else."

Cave 6: Runaway Love

We are finally coming to one of the most important caves of this journey, and that's when I decided to rededicate my life to God. I grew up with this misconception that growing up in church would be my salvation as I grew older. I had stopped attending church during college and afterwards because I felt like I needed to explore life. I got bored with living the good girl life, but the thirstiness of being away from God's presence made me run back to his arms like a toddler in need of rescue.

Sometimes, we think we know what we want or imagine that the world can provide us with greater. In actuality, nothing is GREATER than Him! I ran away from my first true love and my entire being was crying out for God to restore me. I decided that it was time for me to find a church home, and I visited church for over a year. Every day I felt myself getting stronger and found His love surrounding me again. I was no longer running from His love. He wanted me. Not just half of me, but ALL of me, even the broken, ugliest parts of my story. I experienced a transformation coming over me, and I started to lose interest in things that would have me yearning to go back to my past.

One day, I found myself in a service and feeling aligned and connected with the Holy Spirit. Towards the end of the service, I remember being called down to the front of the congregation, and the Man of God spoke a Word into my life that changed the trajectory of my story.

After that moment, I released every chain, every ounce of doubt and every stronghold on that altar. Freedom was now a part of my portion in life and being able to be free in God was the most beautiful feeling I've ever felt. God was what I was actually seeking while I was chasing that high off of the men, the validation and even myself. Having to divorce the old version of myself, yet still remember where I came from was one of the biggest challenges of this season. It wasn't an easy task because it reminded me of who I used to be, and it made me feel as if I was unworthy of the change I needed to better myself.

During this time, I also lost old friendships and mindsets towards life and myself. Looking back on it now, making the decision to change SAVED me from me. It saved my life, and I would do it over and over. Forever. What a true LOVE I found in God! He was the only one who could see my hot tail of a mess life as precious in His sight.

Sharing this with you now brings tears to my eyes because I don't know where I would be if I had not given my life back to God. Maybe I would be strung out on drugs, in a mental institution, or pregnant and alone on the streets out here heartless in this cold world, BUT GOD!

How could I continue to run away from the very reason I have breath in my body? God needed me back in his arms, but I had to be willing to receive His Love. Majority of the time we run away from things we can't comprehend, and I couldn't understand how God could still choose me despite all of my dirt. The beauty of running away is you can always find your way back home or in this case back in the embrace of God.

I don't know who needs to hear this, but you are NOT the last drink you had. You are NOT the last person you slept with. You are NOT the last fire you experienced because that doesn't define you. You are who God calls you to be, and you are fearfully and wonderfully made in his sight. You are worthy to be LOVED by Him, and He isn't embarrassed by any petty mistake you might be involved in. I have been there, and I know how you're feeling, but God can erase every feeling of uncertainty about how you think he will view you. We will talk more about my journey through and to Christ further in the caves. This was the beginning of my walk with Christ.

Let this set of affirmations shower you with God's love as you say them aloud.

Affirmations:

"I WILL always remember that I can never run too far away from God's love."

"I WILL find comfort that God is waiting for me to come home."

Cave 7: Blurred Lines

Now, that I had found Christ, you would think that life got sweeter and all of my problems washed away, right? I thought so too, but this next cave had me in a weird space. Life as I knew it was slowly being stripped away from me because I wanted to do better, but I kept finding myself looking back.

I constantly compared how the good yet toxic times were more enjoyable than now. The thing is if it didn't involve drama and toxicity, it didn't excite me so I downplayed it. This time period felt like I was intoxicated and stumbling all over life again. The danger of living life without direction is that you can become confused on where you should be headed. I was in the care of the best driver, which was God, but I wanted to act like I knew the best route for my life.

I was living life based on yesterday and neglecting the blessing of today. Don't get reared into believing that your past is the best your life has to offer. Your future is too bright to live in the shadows of your past. The only thing I can recall during this time is being a teacher and it became one of the best decisions I ever made.

At the time I was having a difficult time getting a job in the major I went to college for, but I knew I enjoyed working with children. So, one day I decided to apply for a few positions and two months later I received a call about starting my journey as an educator. I didn't have the qualifications, but I was naturally drawn to nurturing the minds of these amazing human beings.

Listen, in times where you're trying to rediscover yourself you have to find something in life that brings you purpose and operate out of that space instead of the blurred confusion of who you were in the past. Purpose will make you become more intentional with your focus, and you will be more present throughout that discovery process.

Affirmations:

"I WILL remain present in life even if situations aren't to my liking."

"I WILL cherish every moment of the time I'm blessed to breathe."

Cave 8: Get It Together Love

Hopefully, the last cave showed the importance of "living" instead of existing in life because years can pass without you having anything to show for it. Time for us to grab our gear, and I want to give you a few tools for the adventures in this next part of the cave. Take note of these words: Accountability, Attitude, Focus and Permission. Each of these tools helped me start enjoying life again, and my hope is that they do the same for you.

The years 2017 until now were when I finally stopped feeling sorry for myself. I made an intentional decision to GET IT TOGETHER. At the time I was in between temp jobs because I was still having a hard time landing a job in my field I went to college for. One of my first real jobs was being a Call Center Specialist for three years, and whew! It definitely wasn't meant for the faint of heart. During that time, I also called myself attending graduate school because of the pressure to have a title and feel like I made it.

Listen, the one thing nobody warned me of before I started that job and enrolled in graduate school was not to allow anyone or anything to make me take on obligations that I didn't feel God was telling me to do. The next thing I knew, I found myself quitting my job and eventually walking away from my graduate program.

This part of the cave is a vital piece that would play a role in me finding my why and true purpose for existing on this planet. For years I lived my life off the opinions of what others thought I should do. It was liberating to take strides towards what brought me joy.

For example, my previous journey of teaching taught me so much about myself. I learned about my compassion, dreams, love, patience, and selflessness. The relationships I built with my former students brought so much life during the season where I literally felt lifeless.

Was it easy? HECK NAH! I experienced the GOOD, BAD and REAL UGLY, but the life changing moments that my students had were the rewards I cherished the most! The following tools were daily mantras I taught my students as tools to utilize, and I started to implement them into my life as well.

The first tool was accountability, and it's usually a big one we try to purposefully avoid. Throughout this entire quest until now, I refused to take responsibility for my involvement in each cave. It wasn't that I didn't want to, but I didn't know how to.

Accountability reveals your maturity level and it's an important ingredient to your healing. Now, you don't have to keep moving in life feeling guilty or ashamed for the parts you played, but it is important to just own up to what you contributed to those situations.

The second tool is attitude, and like the great saying goes, “Your attitude will determine your altitude.” In every cave experience we’ve gone through I had a negative attitude and that will create a breeding ground for negative experiences. This made me realize that I was the problem, and I needed to change. Once you shift your attitude about yourself and life, you will attract more of the pleasant moments you want to experience.

The third tool is focus, and wherever your focus goes your energy goes. I struggled with aligning my focus on what truly matters for years, and it left a trail of regret behind. The day I shifted my focus, I witnessed a shift in my life as well. Focus on what will build you up and help you illuminate the treasure within. If it is not beneficial to you, then don't waste another day of your energy on it.

Finally, the last tool is permission. Overall, nothing has control over us without our permission. I noticed that I allowed life to take over the steering wheel, and I gladly hopped in for the ride. You have to give yourself permission to forgive yourself, permission to release and permission to walk an unfamiliar path to become the best version of yourself.

As we take our last steps out of the discovery of my personal Mine through relationship and self-confidence battles, I want to leave you with these last few gems, and prayerfully this tour has given you the opportunity to and to rediscover the treasure that's within you too.

You are never too damaged to shine in the midst of darkness, and guess what? That's the best time to dig even deeper to unveil the greatness within your Mine. It's been a pleasure having you on this treasure hunt with me. So, what are you waiting for? It's time to start digging your way out of your own Mine!

Affirmations:

"I WILL continue to work on the overall betterment of myself."

"I WILL utilize accountability, attitude, focus and permission properly in my life to build me and not to destroy me."

"I WILL cherish and protect the treasure within my Mine and allow it to shine as a testament for others."

"I WILL live an intentional life and be unashamed to welcome enjoyment."

"I WILL seek God regarding my life's calling."

"I WILL welcome growth into my space."

About the Author

Songbirds are meant to fly and vocal artist, Ranikka J.,is spreading her wings and following her dreams.

Born in Little Rock,Arkansas but raised in the southern town of Pine Bluff, Arkansas, Ranikka J. is the perfect blend of southern hospitality mixed with a vibrant and bold personality. From the age of 2 years old Ranikka has astounded her peers and supporters with her passion and exuberance for life through singing and vocal performance.

In 2013, Ranikka graduated with her Bachelor's Degree in Biology/Pre-Medicine from The University of Arkansas At Pine Bluff. She was also classically trained as a member of the world-renowned Vesper Choir. That experience helped to perfect the expression of her voice into the soulful melodies she can be found sharing today. Her greatest musical inspirations include artists such as: Whitney Houston, Michael Jackson, The Clark Sisters, Chaka Khan, Brandy, Lauryn Hill, Beyoncé just to name a few. Each of these artists have aided Ranikka into tapping into the essence of her own vibe and personal style of singing.

Currently, Ranikka is passionately pursuing her dreams of being a full-time artist. She has now added author to her resume. Writing has always been an outlet for Ranikka to express her thoughts freely through journaling and songwriting. Her desire is to activate the inner writer within those who come across her stories and encourage them to release their truths unapologetically.

When it comes to songwriting, she aims to provide a voice of comfort and songs of fortitude, strength and magnetic energy to audiences across the globe. Her true mission is to be a female lyrical artist that engages the emotional appeal of those who truly enjoy passion and truth in music.

Ranikka says, “I want to empower generations and illustrate a new sense of respect amongst ourselves while also depicting the depths of our hearts and minds. Soulful music for the new age era! I want to be relatable to all ethnicity groups, age groups as well as all genres. This allows me to motivate and empower the world through song. Lastly, I’ll be able to continue to deliver a poetic, lyrical and meaningful notion through music.”

Today, Ranikka J. can be found inspiring her audiences through thought provoking and inspirational creations. She creatively collaborates with engaging artists across the globe while performing her latest releases for her audience.

To stay updated with this Songbirds journey, connect with her across all social platforms @RanikkaJ.

www.ingramcontent.com/pod-product-compliance
Ingram Content Group UK Ltd.
Pitfield, Milton Keynes, MK11 3LW, UK
UKHW020414250726
13967UKWH00007B/2644
9 781304 668417